MW01463694

This book belongs to:
....

Every animal tries to sleep. Please wish them good night using kind sentences and find out who is not sleeping yet.

© Copyright 2022 - All rights reserved.

You may not reproduce, duplicate or send the contents of this book without direct written permission from the author. You cannot hereby despite any circumstance blame the publisher or hold him or her to legal responsibility for any reparation, compensations, or monetary forfeiture owing to the information included herein, either in a direct or an indirect way.

Legal Notice: This book has copyright protection. You can use the book for personal purpose. You should not sell, use, alter, distribute, quote, take excerpts or paraphrase in part or whole the material contained in this book without obtaining the permission of the author first.

Disclaimer Notice: You must take note that the information in this document is for casual reading and entertainment purposes only.
We have made every attempt to provide accurate, up to date and reliable information. We do not express or imply guarantees of any kind. The persons who read admit that the writer is not occupied in giving legal, financial, medical or other advice. We put this book content by sourcing various places.

Please consult a licensed professional before you try any techniques shown in this book. By going through this document, the book lover comes to an agreement that under no situation is the author accountable for any forfeiture, direct or indirect, which they may incur because of the use of material contained in this document, including, but not limited to, — errors omissions, or inaccuracies.

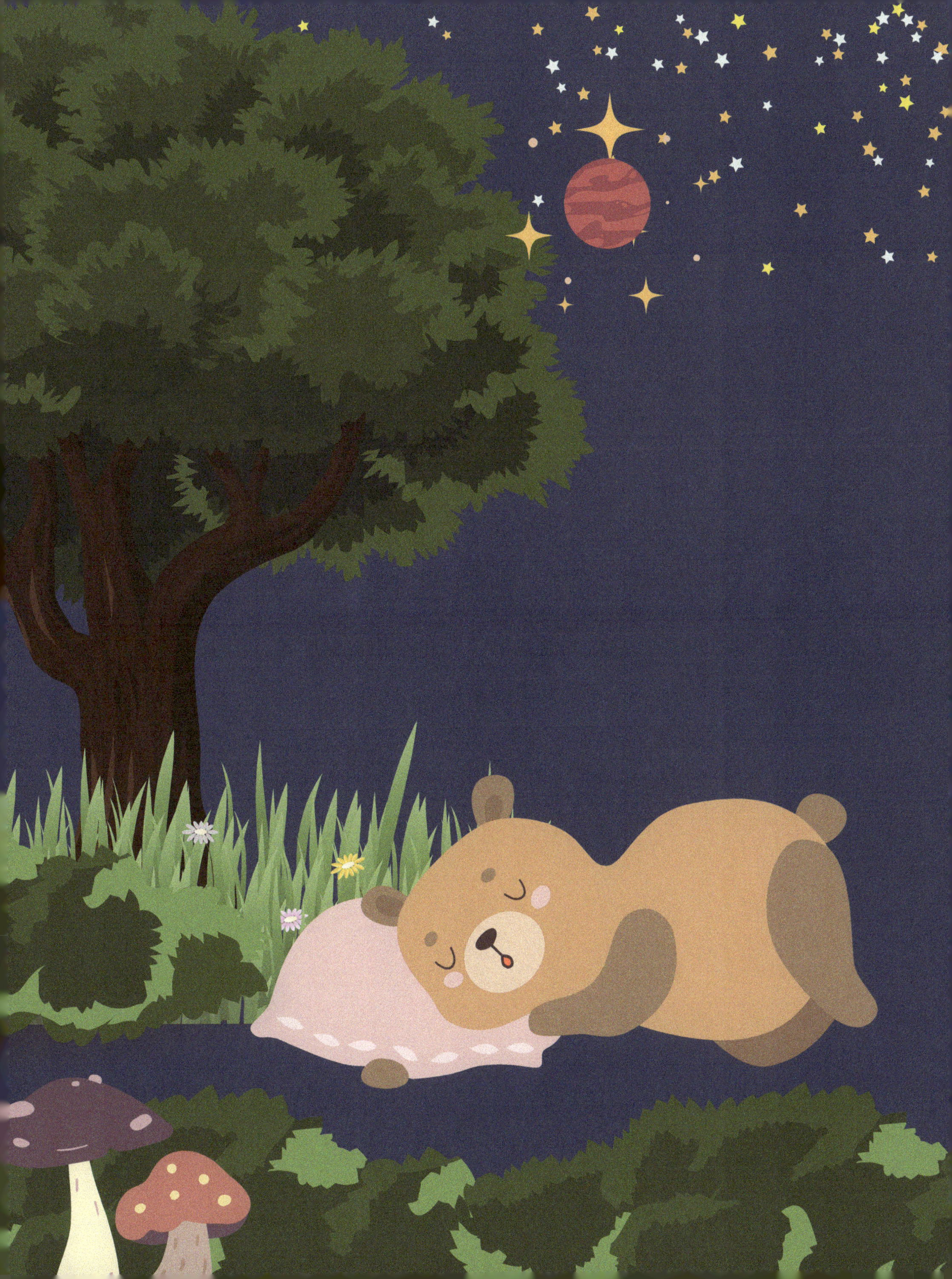

Good night bear,
Sleep well!

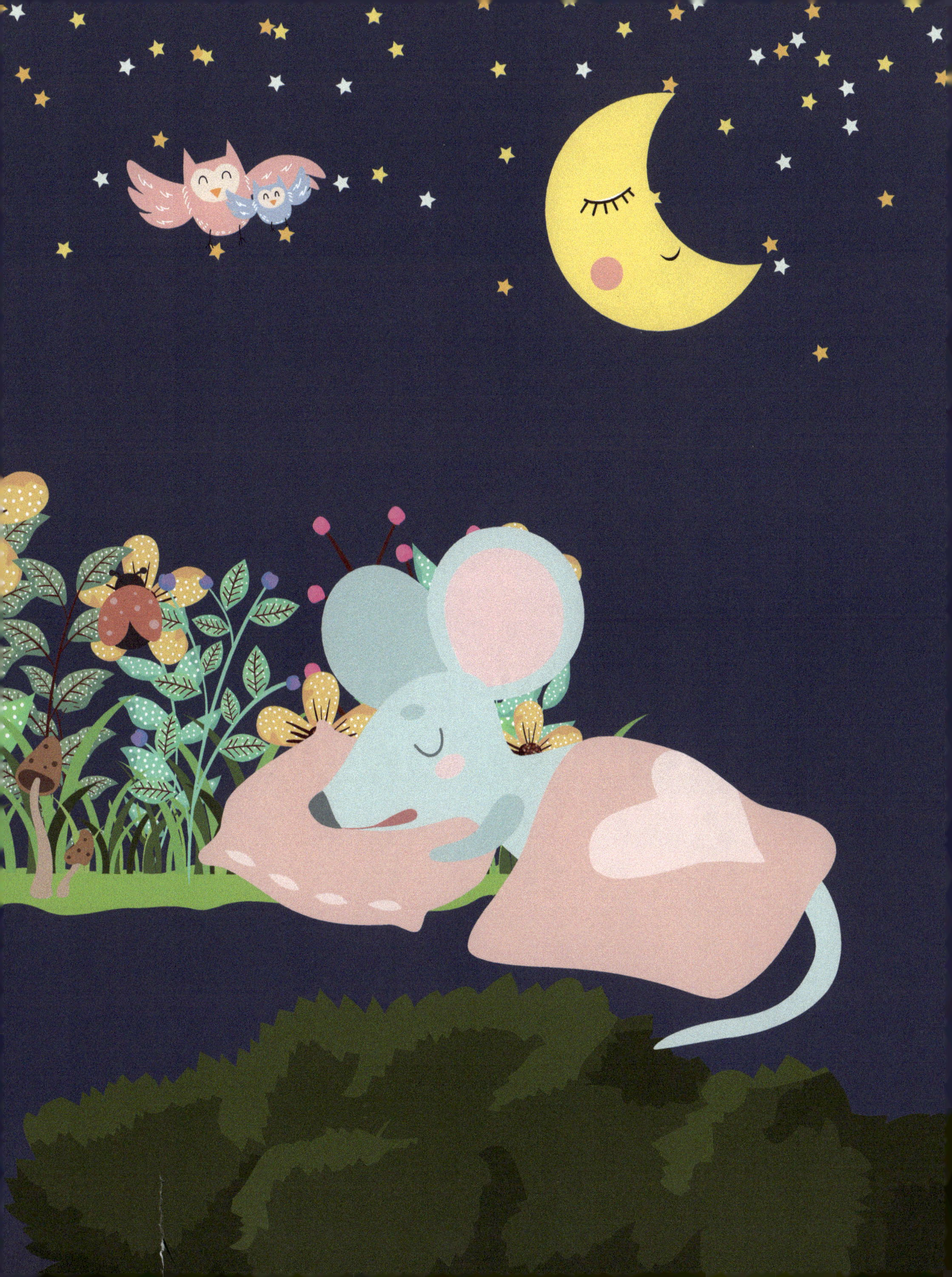

Good night mouse,
I like your nose.

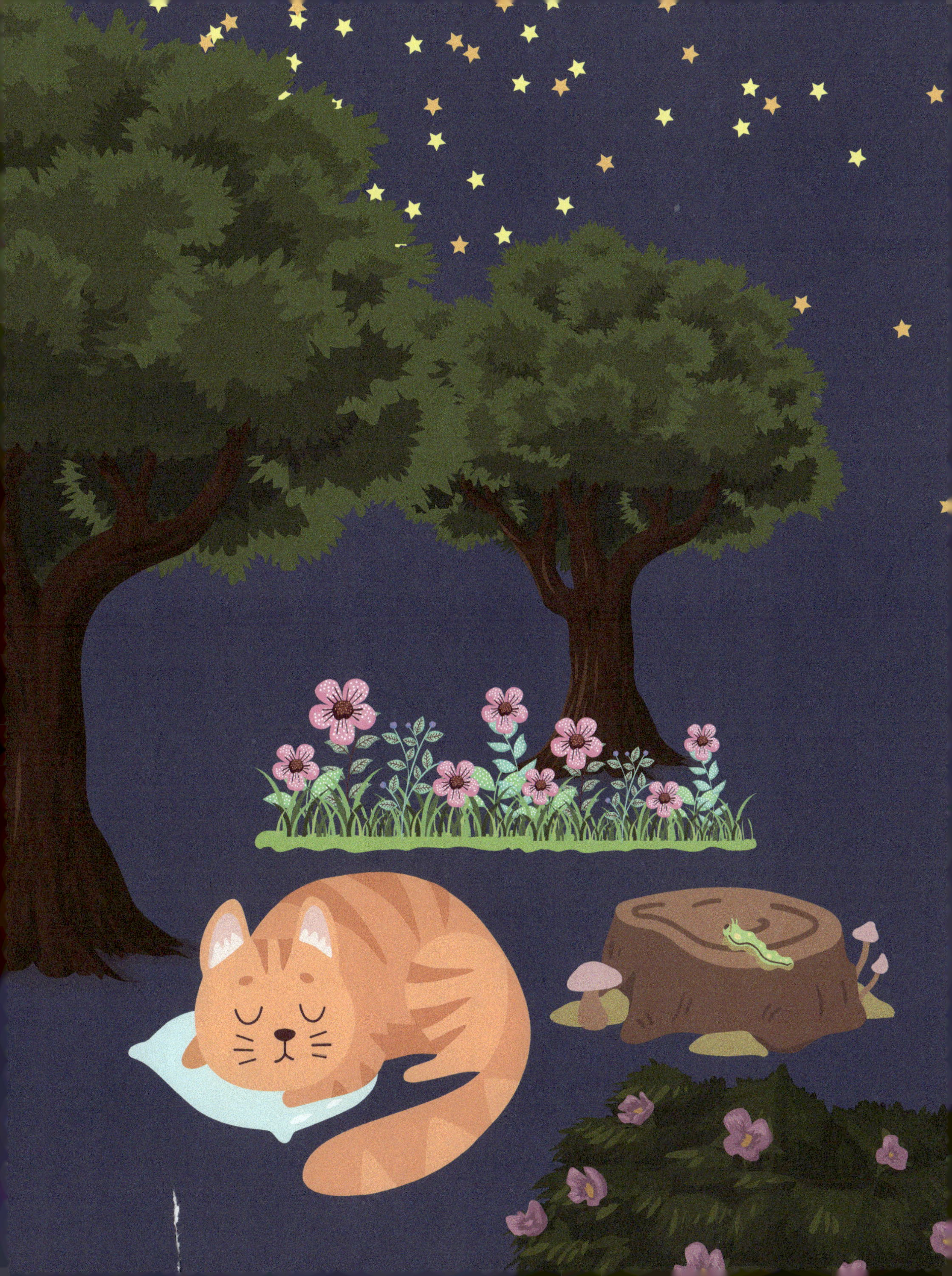

Good night cat,
Please tomorrow
Do not be sad.

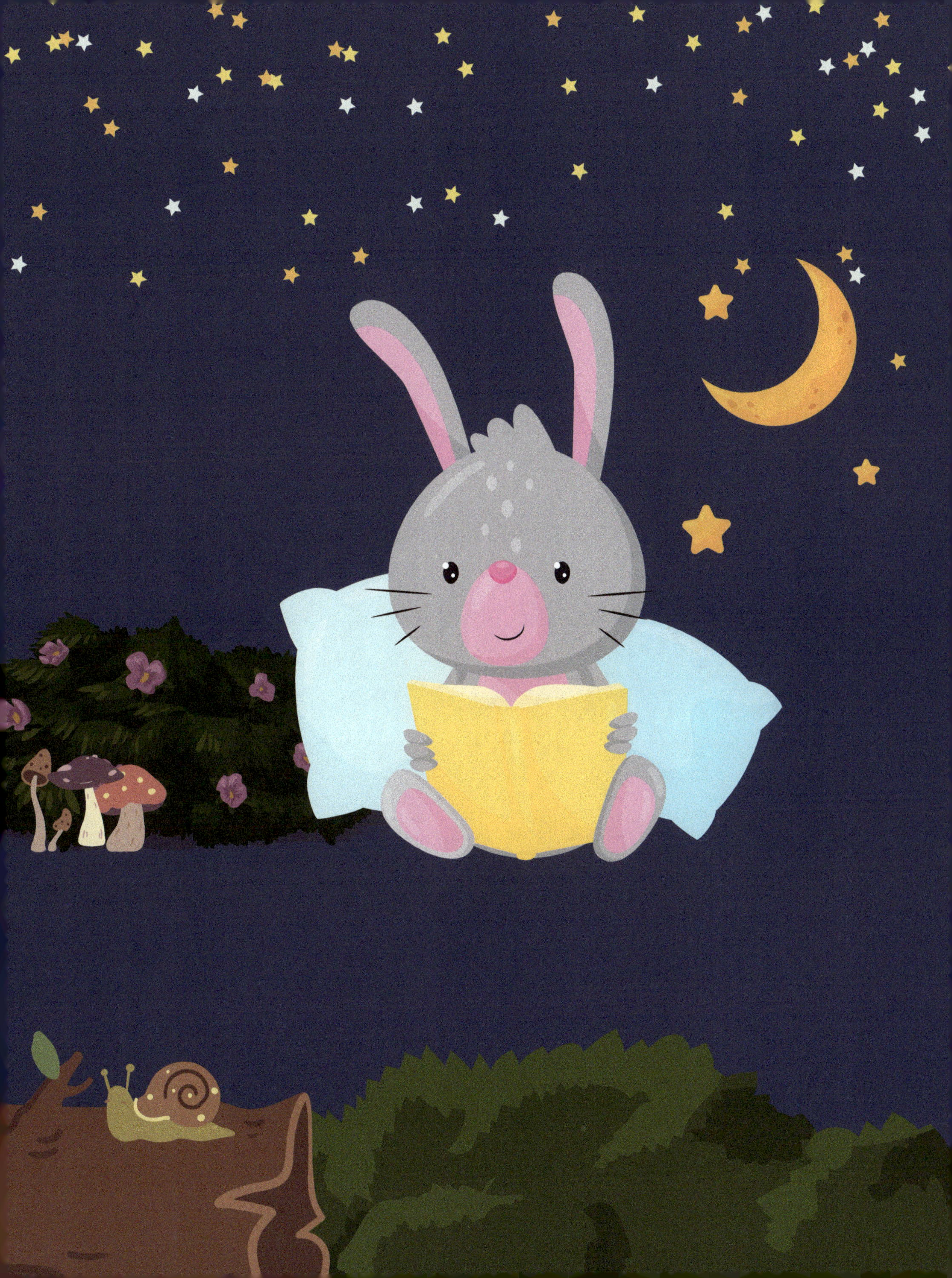

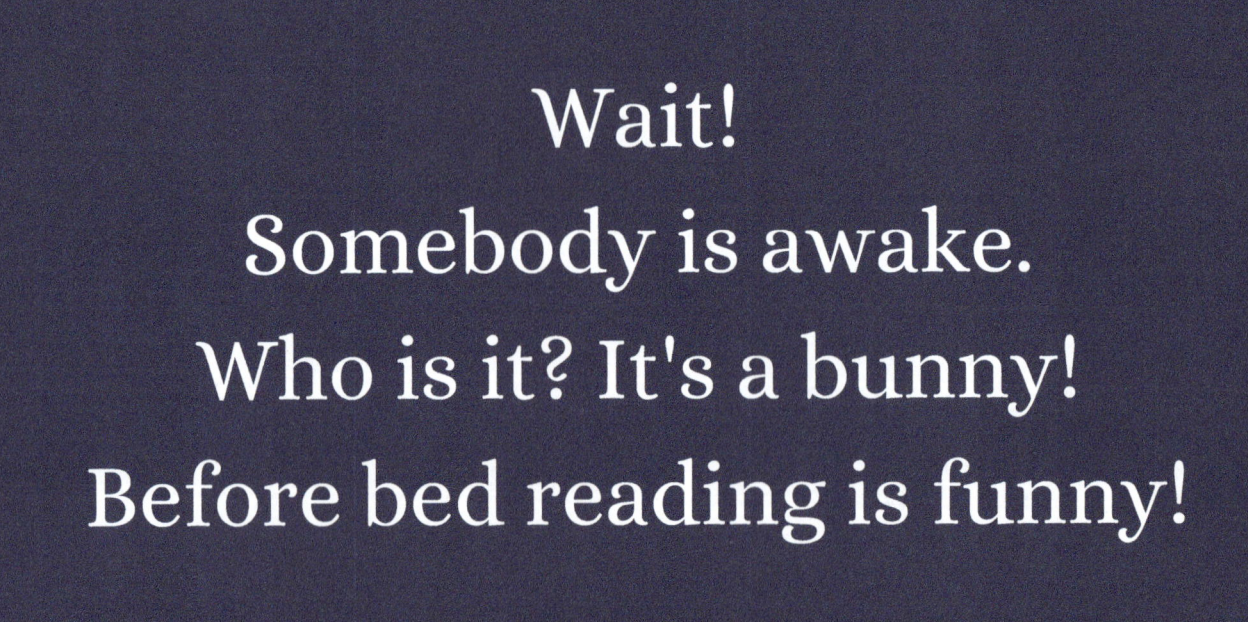

Wait!
Somebody is awake.
Who is it? It's a bunny!
Before bed reading is funny!

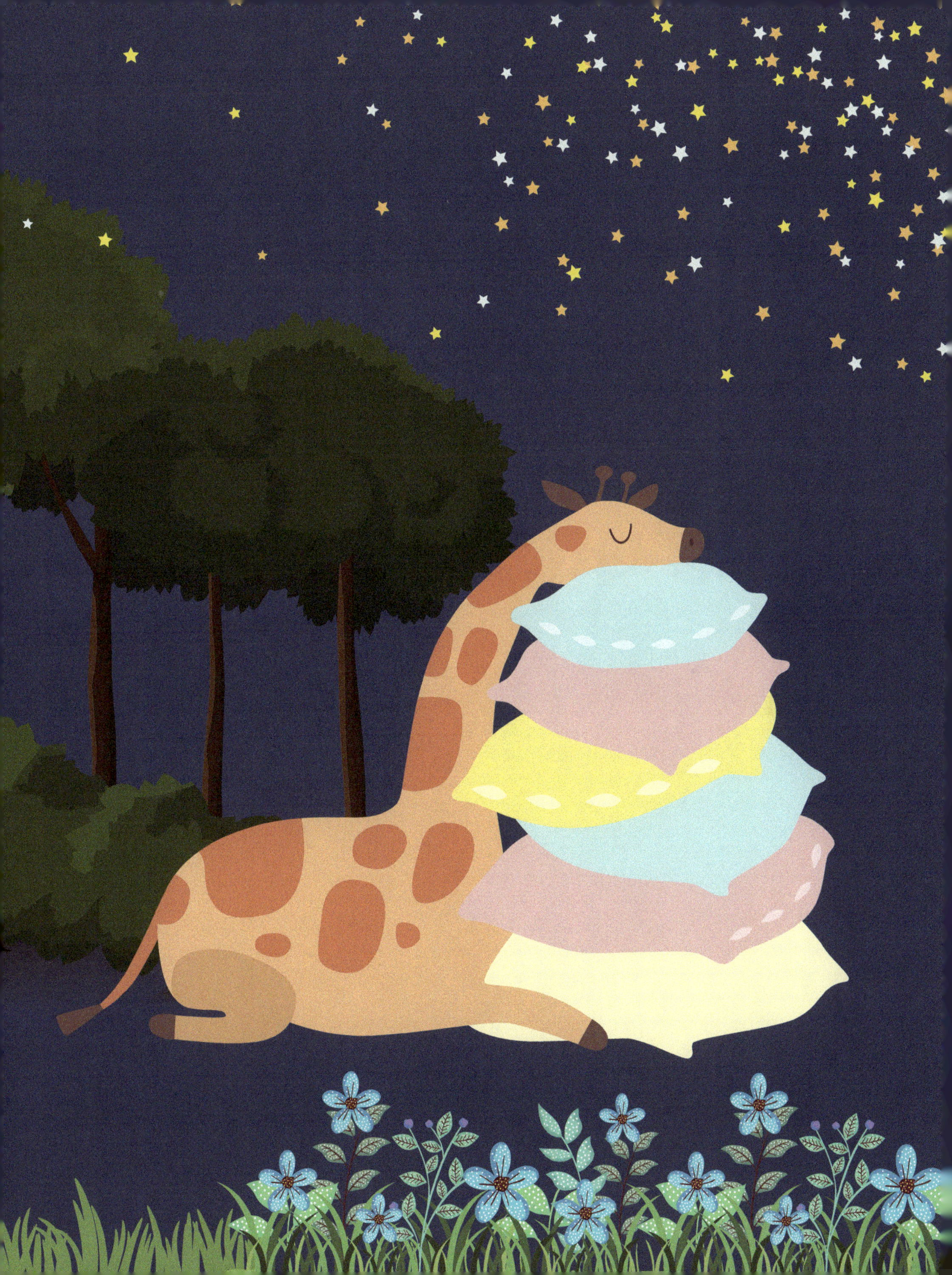

Sleep well giraffe,
This is a very good night.

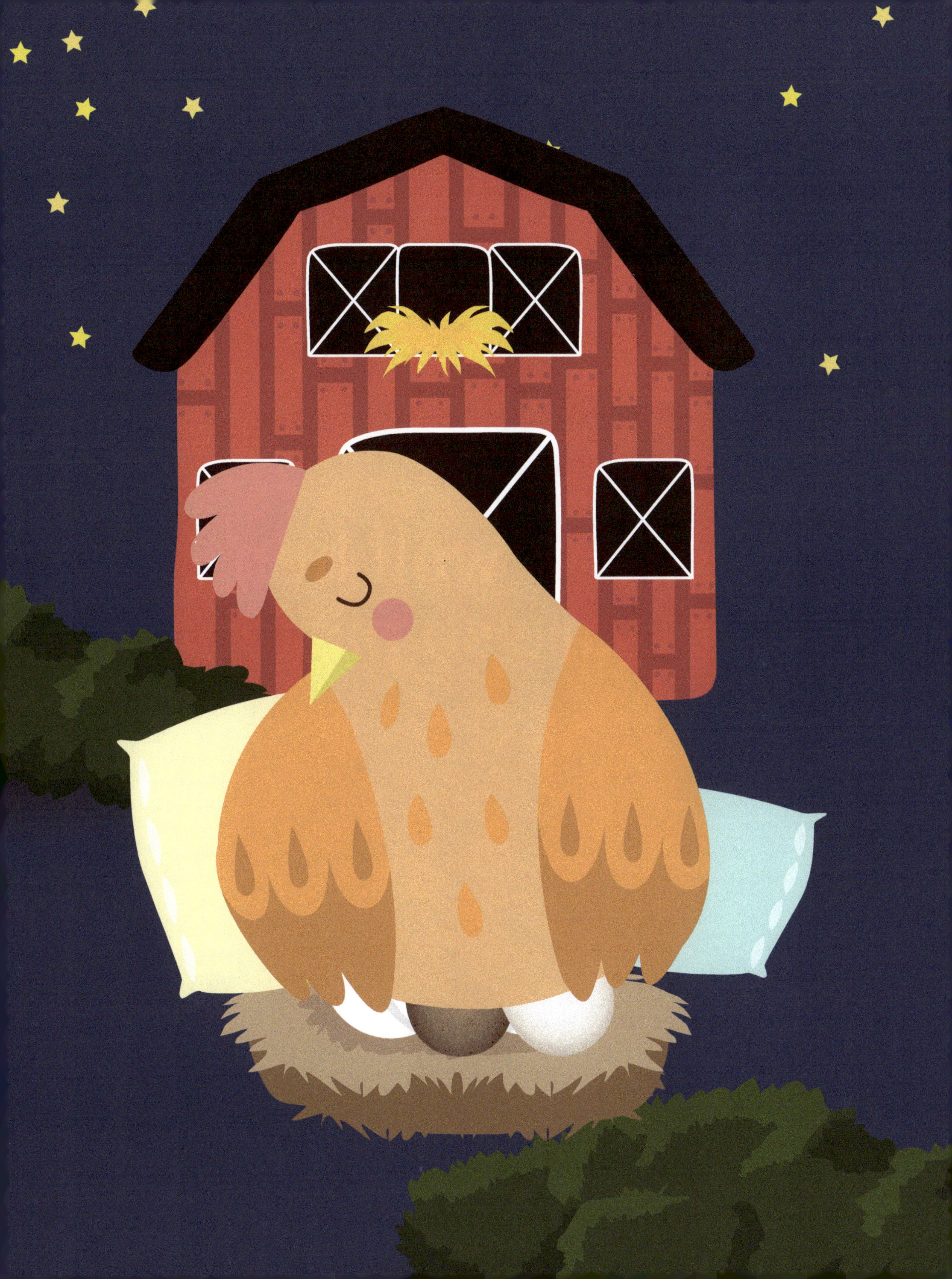

Sleep well hen,
You are so patient.

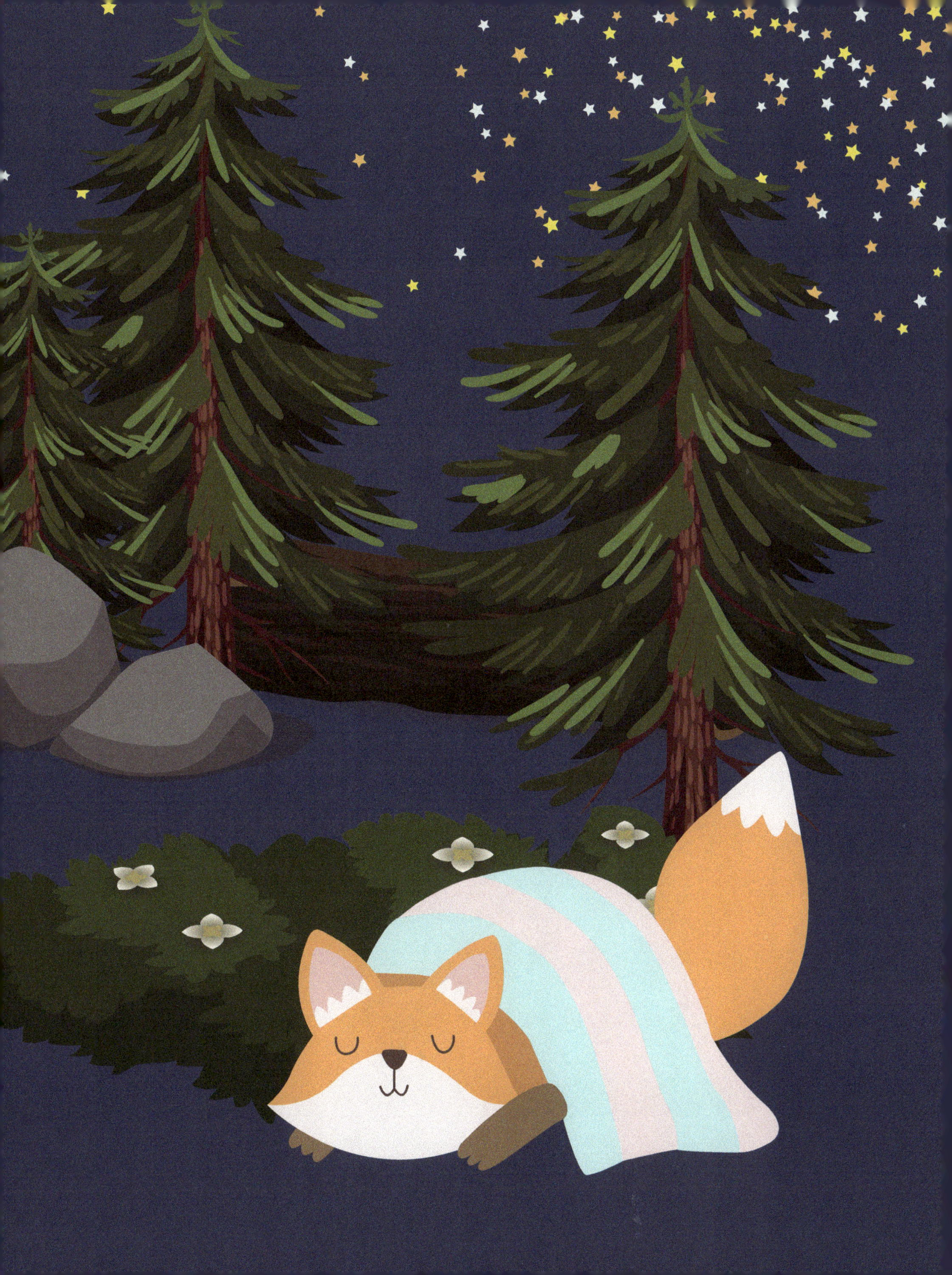

Good night fox,
You are so generous.

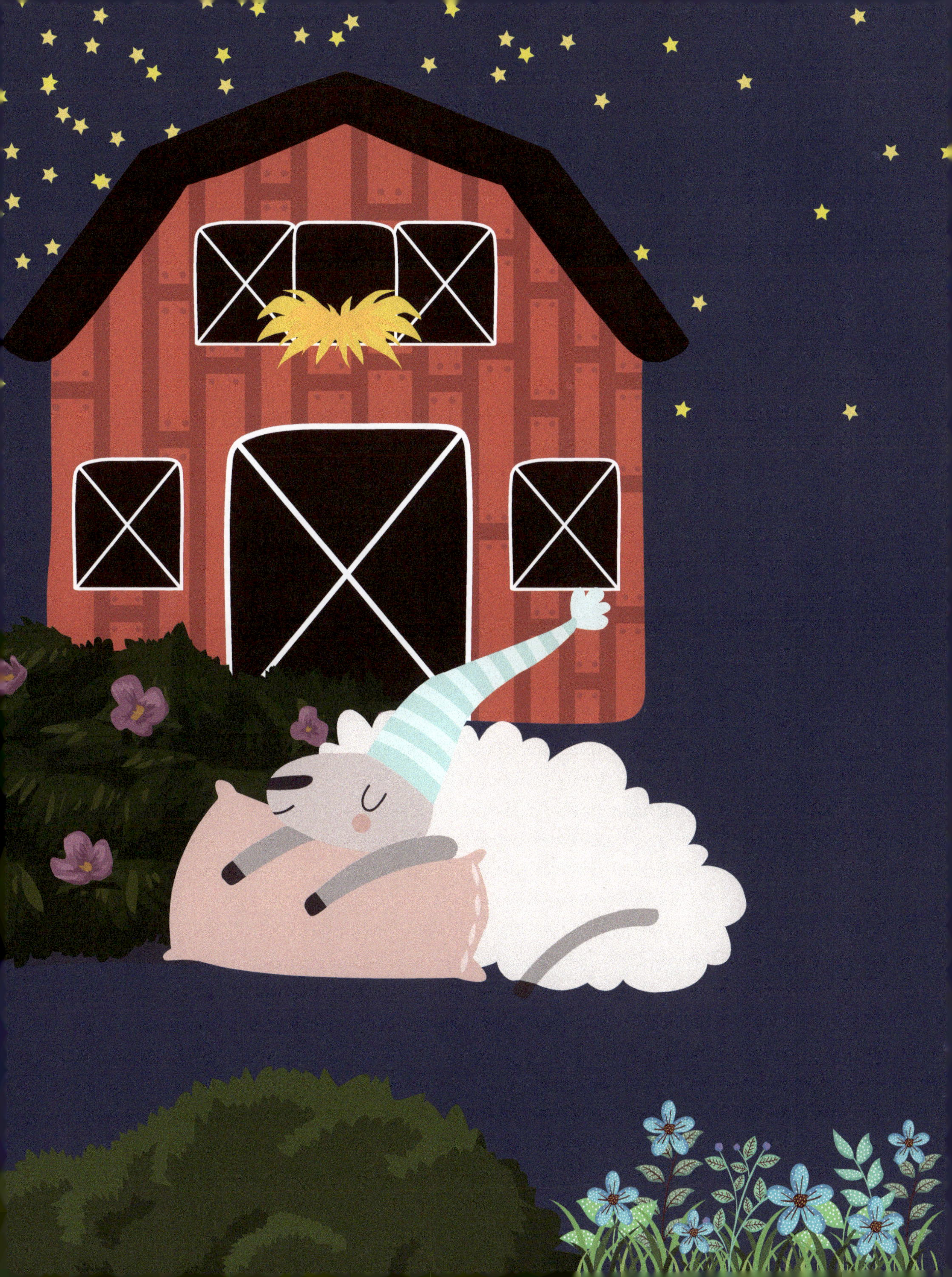

Good night sheep, sheep,
You sleep so deep, deep.

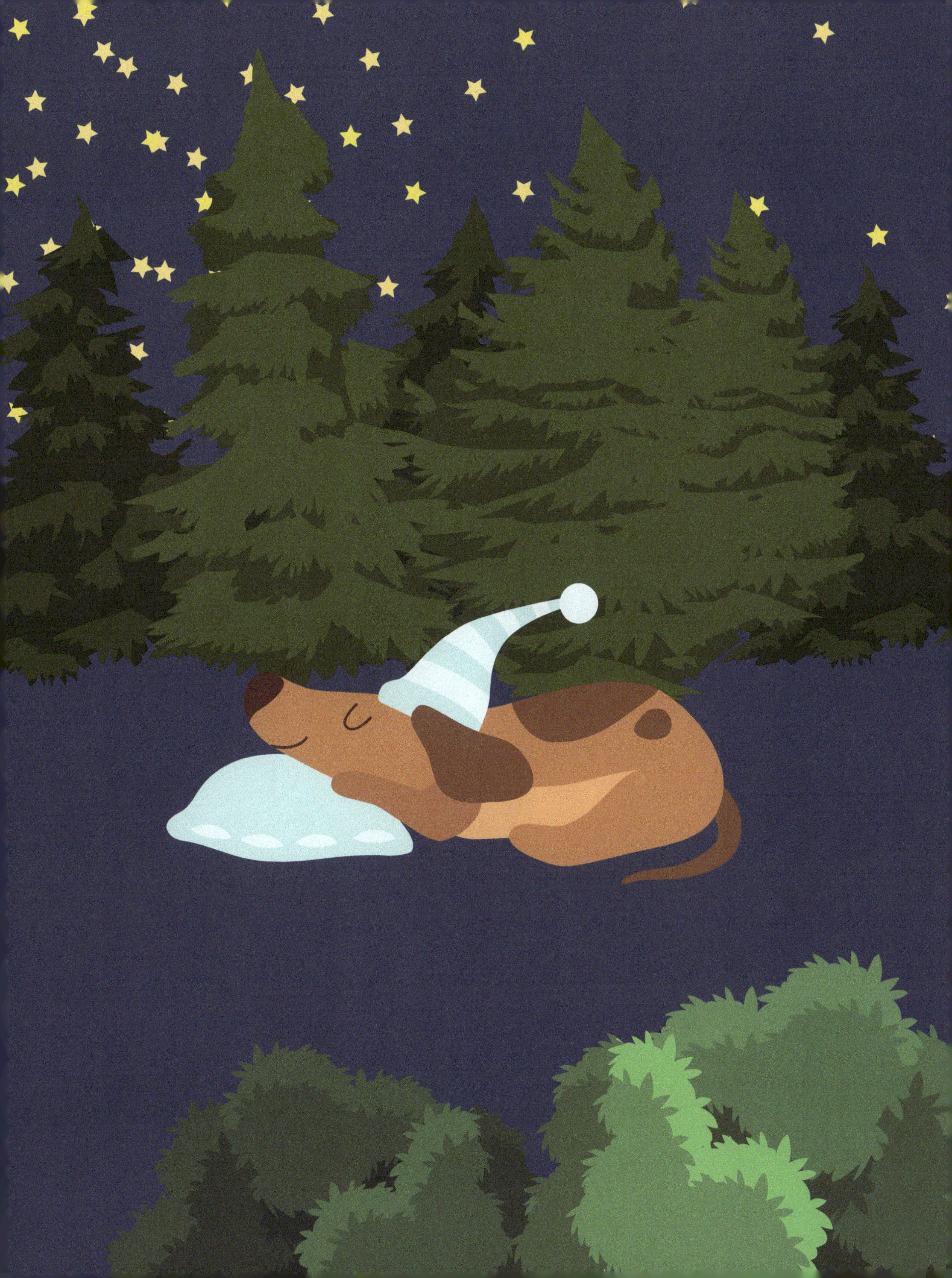

Good night dog,
You are so cute.

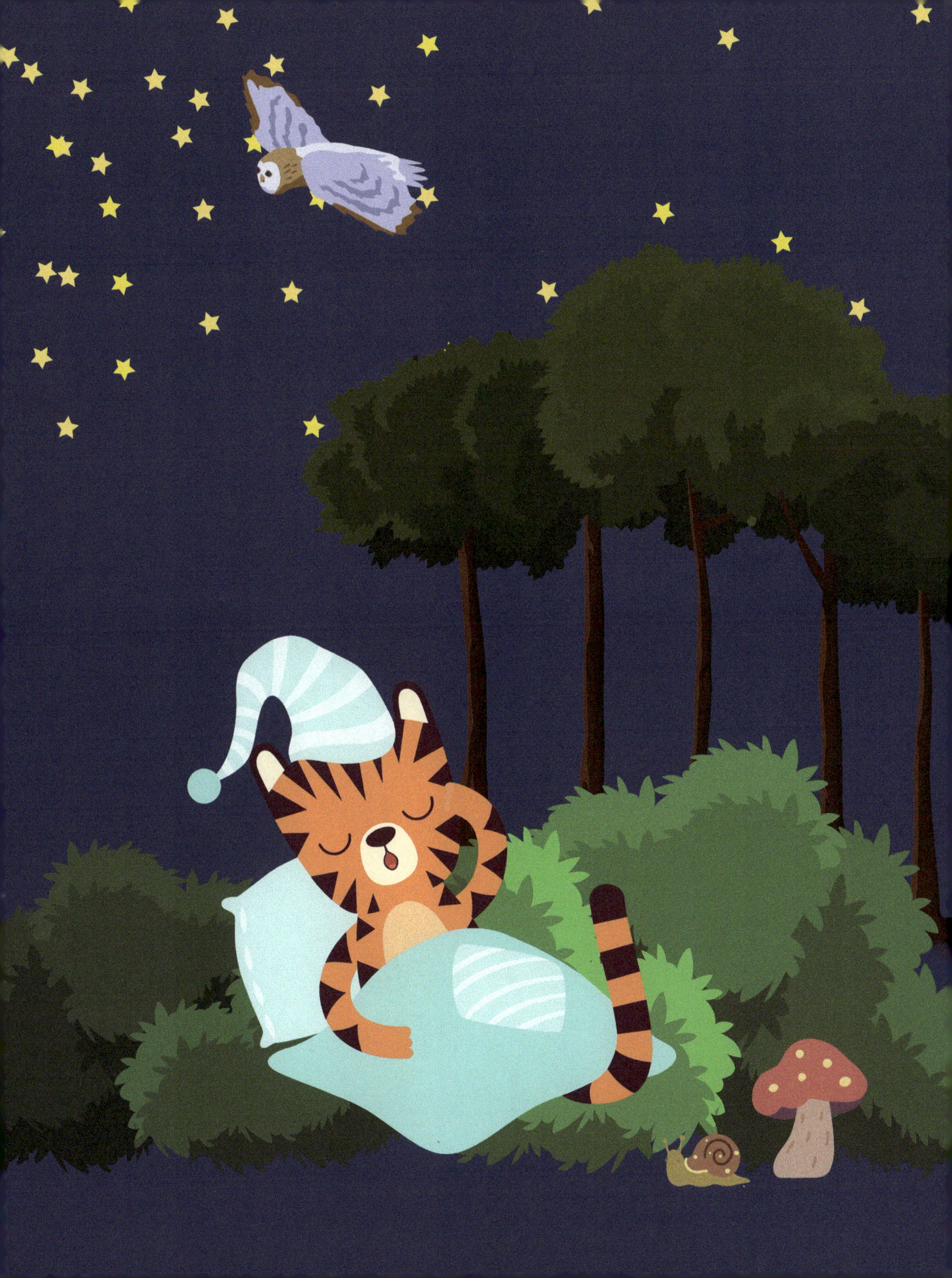

Good night tiger,
You are the strongest.

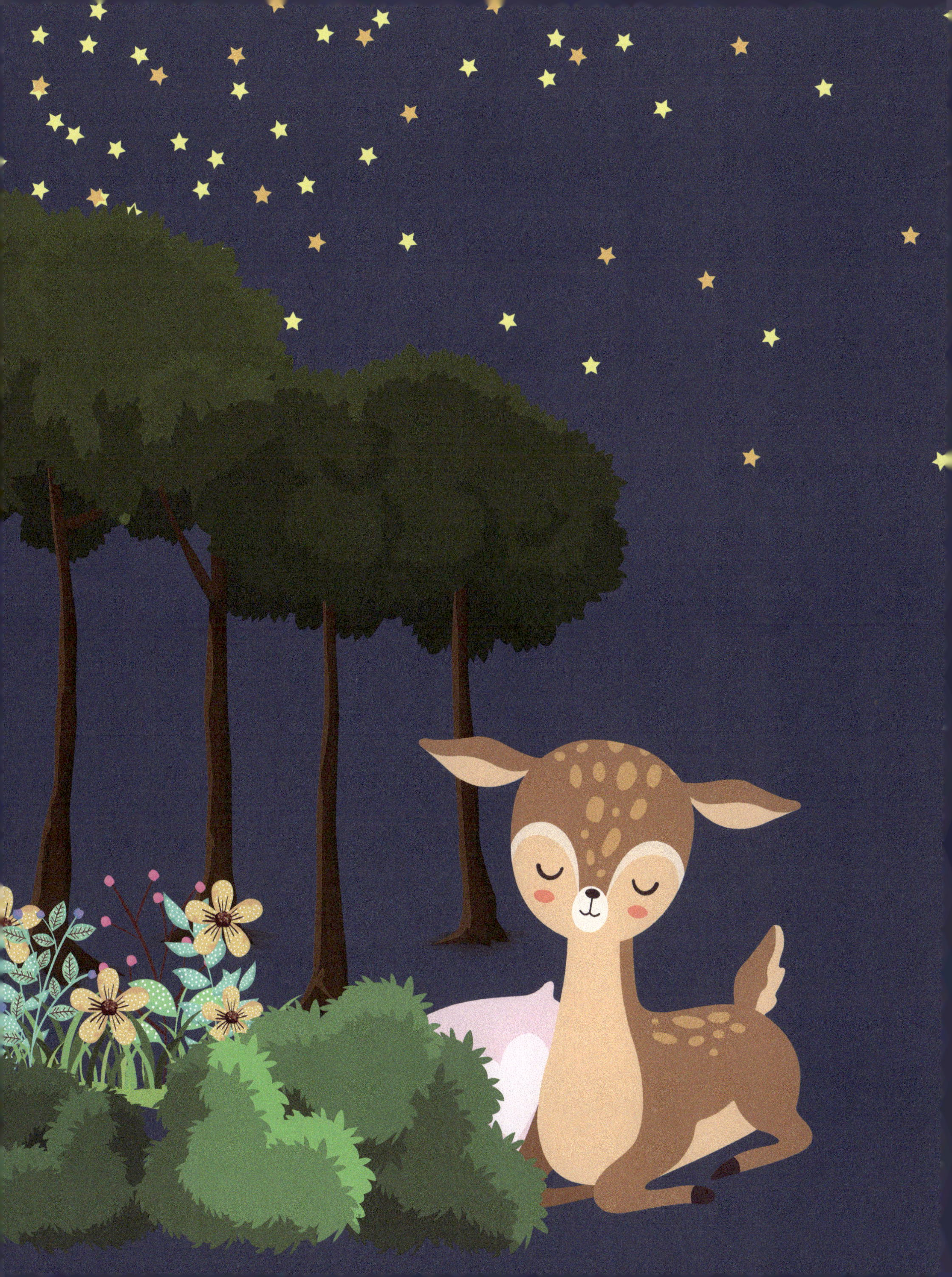

Sleep well deer,
We will meet
tomorrow here.

Good night moon and good night stars. Good night everybody after all!

Wait! Someone is still awake!
Who is it? You are!
Night, Night!
Do not forget to turn off the
Light, light!

Thank you!

We hope you enjoyed our book.
Our customers are very important to us!

As a small family business, please share your feedback with us at the address below:

notebook.publish@gmail.com

CPSIA information can be obtained
at www.ICGtesting.com
Printed in the USA
BVHW021202050522
636222BV00045BA/1272

9 783755 115229